Bald Eagle Nest Survey Katmai National Park & Preserve, Alaska

Natural Resource Data Series NPS/KATM/NRDS—2011/311

Leslie A. Witter

National Park Service
Southwest Alaska Network
Lake Clark National Park & Preserve
1 Park Place
Port Alsworth, Alaska 99653

Sherri A. Anderson

National Park Service
Katmai National Park & Preserve
#1 King Salmon Mall
P.O. Box 7
King Salmon, Alaska 99613

October 2011

U.S. Department of the Interior
National Park Service
Natural Resource Stewardship and Science
Fort Collins, Colorado

The National Park Service, Natural Resource Stewardship and Science office in Fort Collins, Colorado publishes a range of reports that address natural resource topics of interest and applicability to a broad audience in the National Park Service and others in natural resource management, including scientists, conservation and environmental constituencies, and the public.

The Natural Resource Data Series is intended for the timely release of basic data sets and data summaries. Care has been taken to assure accuracy of raw data values, but a thorough analysis and interpretation of the data has not been completed. Consequently, the initial analyses of data in this report are provisional and subject to change.

All manuscripts in the series receive the appropriate level of peer review to ensure that the information is scientifically credible, technically accurate, appropriately written for the intended audience, and designed and published in a professional manner.

This report received informal peer review by subject-matter experts who were not directly involved in the collection, analysis, or reporting of the data. Data in this report were collected and analyzed using methods based on established, peer-reviewed protocols and were analyzed and interpreted within the guidelines of the protocols.

Views, statements, findings, conclusions, recommendations, and data in this report do not necessarily reflect views and policies of the National Park Service, U.S. Department of the Interior. Mention of trade names or commercial products does not constitute endorsement or recommendation for use by the U.S. Government.

This report is available from the Natural Resource Publications Management website (http://www.nature.nps.gov/publications/nrpm/).

Please cite this publication as:

NPS 127/110710, October 2011

Contents

Figures

Tables

Abstract

Nest occupancy and reproductive success of the large breeding populations of bald eagles (*Haliaeetus leucocephalus*) within parks in the Southwest Alaska Network (SWAN), including Katmai National Park & Preserve (KATM), have been selected as a "vital sign" for monitoring as they are indicative of the health of both freshwater and marine ecosystems. Records of nesting activity were collected from 1974-1997 in KATM, but monitoring lapsed from 1998-2010. In 2011, we reinitiated eagle surveys in KATM following a standardized sampling protocol with an initial double-count aerial survey in May to determine nest locations and occupancy, and a follow-up survey in July to assess productivity. Objectives of this report were to: (1) map all empty and incubating eagle nests located in the Naknek drainage of KATM in 2011, (2) summarize historic KATM bald eagle nesting data, and (3) discuss techniques that can be used for future consistent monitoring. We found 33 incubating and 25 empty nests in the Naknek drainage in 2011. Nest success was 62%, with 0.90 ± 0.15 SE chicks per incubating nest. The number of incubating nests in the Naknek area was higher than any number recorded in the past. Reproductive success fell within the range of past productivity rates, and is indicative of a healthy and stable population. Monitoring trends in bald eagle nest occupancy and productivity over time will allow us to gauge when broader natural or human-caused changes may be occurring within KATM ecosystems.

Acknowledgments

Vera Gilliland, Troy Hamon, and Neal Labrie provided invaluable logistical support in KATM. Thanks to Jose de Creeft (Northwind Aviation) and Allen Gilliland (NPS – KATM) for their excellent piloting skills and assistance with eagle observations. We thank Buck Mangipane (NPS – LACL) for help creating an ESRI ArcPad application for use in KATM surveys. Thanks to Claudette Moore (NPS – KATM) and Susan Savage (USFWS) for their assistance locating sources of past Katmai eagle survey data. We appreciate review comments by Heather Coletti (NPS – SWAN), Laura Phillips (NPS – KEFJ), and Susan Savage (USFWS) that greatly improved this report. The project was funded by the National Park Service SWAN I&M Program with logistical and staff support provided by KATM.

Acronyms

ALAG   Alagnak Wild River

ANIA   Aniakchak National Monument & Preserve

KATM   Katmai National Park & Preserve

KEFJ   Kenai Fjords National Park

LACL   Lake Clark National Park & Preserve

SWAN   Southwest Alaska Network

USFWS   United States Fish & Wildlife Service

Introduction

Alaska has long been considered a stronghold for bald eagles (*Haliaeetus leucocephalus*). Although a bounty system was in place until 1953 (Hodges et al. 1979), eagle numbers were never reduced to the degree experienced in the contiguous 48 states (USFWS 2009). On the Alaska Peninsula from the Katmai coast south to Unimak Island, the bald eagle population is considered healthy (Savage and Hodges 2006). Both the number of adult eagles and occupied nests increased from 1983 to 2000, and have since remained stable (Savage and Hodges 2000, 2006).

The foundation statement of KATM provides for the protection of "...lakes, ponds, wetlands, rivers and streams that offer diverse aquatic habitats and support a wide range of plants and animals", as well as "opportunities to monitor baseline freshwater systems against which to measure environmental change" (KATM 2009). Bald eagles play an important ecological role as keystone predators of waterbirds and fish (Stalmaster 1987, Armstrong 2008). Success of breeding populations of bald eagles is indicative of the health of both freshwater and marine ecosystems (Stalmaster 1987, Bennett et al. 2006). As such, eagles have been selected as a "vital sign" for monitoring in parks within SWAN (Figure 1), including KATM (Bennett et al. 2006).

Although KATM is relatively pristine, there are potential threats to eagle breeding populations from both within and outside park boundaries. These include mineral extraction, oil spills, increasing human visitation (sport hunting, fishing, ecotourism), lead ingestion and incidental trapping take of wintering birds, and effects on food sources due to harvest of salmon and other fish species (Yurick 1989, Gende et al. 1997, Savage and Hodges 2006). Additionally, breeding success is influenced by natural fluctuations in food availability and spring weather (Swenson et al. 1986, Hansen 1987, Gende et al. 1997, Savage 1997).

Records of bald eagle nesting activity were collected from 1975-1979 and 1983-1997 in KATM (Troyer 1974-1979, Jope 1983-1985, 1987, Dutcher 1986, Sowl 1988, Squibb 1992, Savage 1993a, b, 1994, 1997); however, monitoring has lapsed in recent years. Survey areas and methodology used in the past also varied, making year to year comparisons of eagle productivity difficult in some cases. In 2009, work began in KEFJ to field test a protocol for monitoring eagle productivity (Thompson et al. 2009, Thompson and Phillips 2011). This is based on standardized methodology proposed for use in the contiguous 48 states that incorporates dual-frame sampling with a double-observer component to correct for biases in nest sightability (Haines and Pollock 1998, USFWS 2009, Sauer et al. 2011). Using a modification of the KEFJ protocol, eagle surveys were reinitiated in KATM in spring 2011. Ultimately, the goal is to finalize a rigorous survey design for long-term monitoring that will use nest data from a random sampling of eagle habitats to make inferences about the health of the eagle population parkwide and facilitate comparisons of eagle nest occupancy and productivity between SWAN parks. Objectives of this study were to: (1) collect baseline data on all currently empty and incubating eagle nests within the Naknek drainage, (2) summarize historic KATM bald eagle nesting data, and (3) describe techniques that can be used in KATM for future monitoring efforts.

1

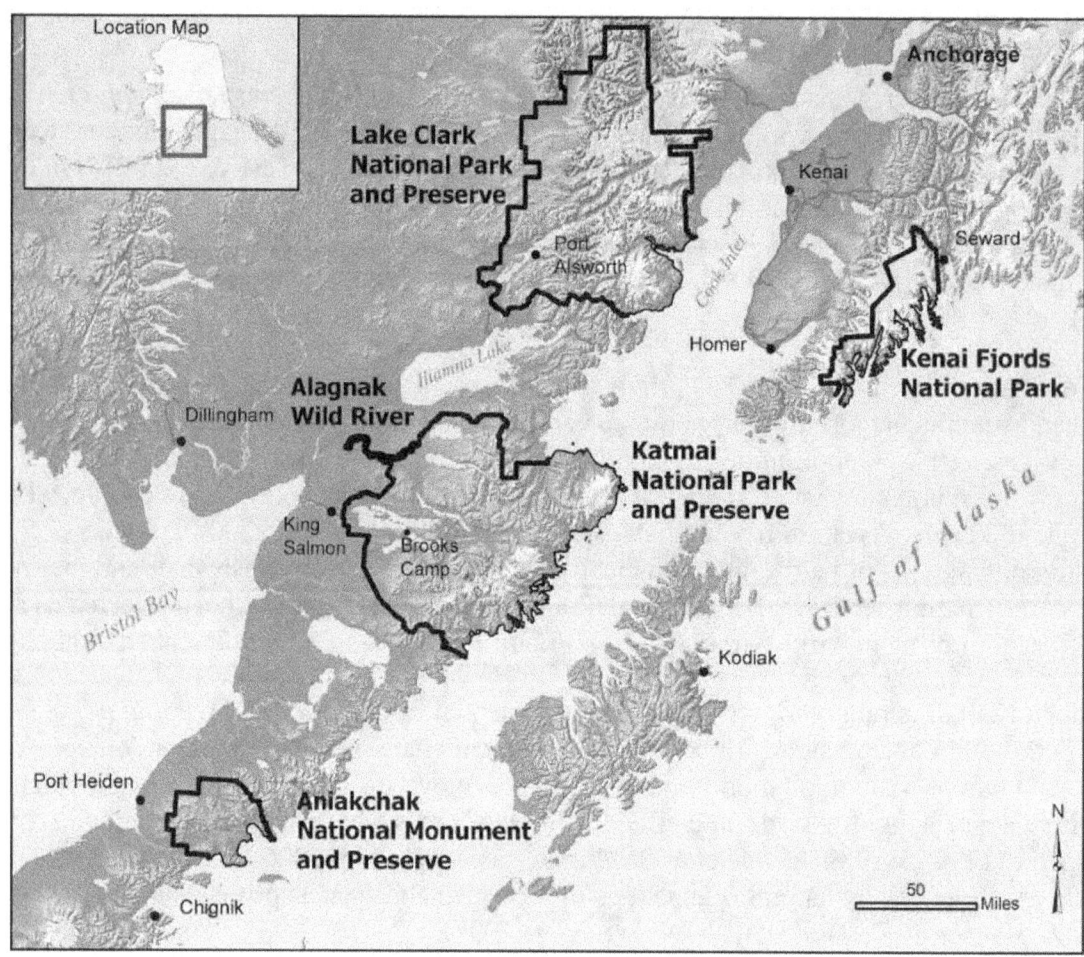

Figure 1. Location of KATM, along with locations of the other four national park units within SWAN (figure from Bennett et al. 2006).

Methods

Study Area

KATM encompasses nearly 20,234 km² (7,813 mi²) at the head of the Alaska Peninsula (Figure 1). The eastern portion of KATM includes 800 km (497 mi) of coastline comprised of narrow fjords and broad coastal flats. Rising to over 2,134 m (7,000 ft), the Aleutian Range separates these coastal areas from the interior of the park to the west. The Lake Region includes Naknek, Brooks, Coville, Grosvenor, Nonvianuk, and Kukaklek Lakes, associated drainages, and foothills in the northwest and central interior of the park. Lowland tundra plains are predominant to the southwest. Vegetation types include boreal forest of white (*Picea alba*) and black spruce (*P. mariana*), birch (*Betula neoalaskana*) and balsam poplar (*Populus balsamifera*) groves, shrublands dominated by willow (*Salix* spp.) and alder (*Alnus* spp.), moist tundra, alpine tundra, and grass/sedge meadows (Troyer 1974, Kozlowski 2007). Climate in the region is transitional between polar and maritime subarctic regimes (Lindsay 2010).

Data Collection

We conducted two aerial surveys during the bald eagle breeding season to determine nest occupancy and productivity in the Naknek Lake drainage of KATM (Figure 2). This drainage area was selected because it has traditionally been the most surveyed area in KATM and includes the majority of bald eagle nesting habitat within the interior of the park. The Naknek Lake drainage encompasses Naknek Lake and all islands, Brooks Lake, the drainage area between Dumpling and Brooks Mountains, the headwaters creek of Brooks Lake (to 7 miles upstream), Margot Creek, Savonoski River (until Grosvenor River), Grosvenor River, Lake Grosvenor, Lake Coville, and American Creek (until it bends east). Survey methodology was adapted from USFWS (2009) recommendations, as well as from protocols employed in KEFJ since 2009 (Thompson et al. 2009, Thompson and Phillips 2011).

We used a Cessna 305-A (L-19), operated via contract with Northwind Aviation, to conduct an initial survey to determine the location and occupancy of nests on May 28-29, 2011. Due to weather conditions and aircraft availability, survey dates were slightly later than the late April-early May window recommended based on estimated nest initiation dates for the area (USFWS Alaska Peninsula/Becharof NWR 2001). During the survey, we flew at speeds of 120-185 km/hr (65-100 knots) and elevations 46-91 m (150-300 ft) above ground level. The general flight path positioned the plane slightly offshore to see inland from lake and river shorelines. King Salmon airport (58°40'35.38"N, 156°38'55.29"W) was the base of flight operations.

We used a double-observer method to record nest detections while allowing for estimation of the proportion of nests missed by observers (Nichols et al. 2000). The pilot acted as the front-seat observer, with the rear-seat observer positioned directly behind the pilot. Each observer waited until a detected nest was out of view of the other observer before announcing that a nest had been seen; nest detections were assumed to be independent between observers. After detection was announced, the nest was circled to allow verification by both observers and additional data collection. We recorded attributes (Table 1) associated with each nest using ESRI ArcPad 7.1 (ESRI, Inc., Redlands, CA) GIS software loaded on a Panasonic Toughbook (Panasonic Corporation, Osaka, Japan) linked to a Garmin 12XL GPS receiver (Garmin International, Inc., Olathe, KS). This software allowed us to capture a point as we flew directly over each nest. The corresponding GPS location was automatically linked to the point. Care was taken to fly at sufficient elevation above the nest so as not to flush incubating eagles. A Garmin GPSMap 76CSx was used to collect a track log of GPS locations spaced at 5-sec intervals to document flight lines. External antennae were attached to both Garmin units to increase accuracy of GPS locations. At the end of each day of the survey, we downloaded GPS and ArcPad data.

During the second aerial survey (July 19, 2011), we used a Department of Interior (DOI) Cessna 185 with a pilot and two observers to revisit all nests that were classified as "incubating" during the May survey. Direct lines were flown between nests. Once a nest was relocated, the pilot and rear observer independently surveyed the nest for young before consulting each other to determine if counts were consistent. The front seat observer recorded the number of young, chick developmental stage, and number of adults using ArcPad (Table 2). When possible, the rear seat observer photographed nests using a Pentax K200 digital SLR with a Quantaray 100-300mm f/4.5-6.7 autofocus lens (Pentax Corporation, Tokyo, Japan).

Analysis
We used DNR Garmin 5.4.1 (Minnesota Department of Natural Resources, St. Paul, MN) to export Garmin GPS data in ESRI shapefile format. Both Garmin and ArcPad spatial data were based on the North American 1983 geographic coordinate system and the North American datum 1983 Alaska Albers projected coordinate system. Data were brought into ESRI ArcGIS 9.3 for editing, mapping, and basic analysis. For each nest detected during the May survey, we generated a unique identification number (ID) consisting of the USGS 1:63,360 topographic Map Series, Quadrangle, and nest number. Nests within a given quadrangle were numbered consecutively.

We used Microsoft Excel 2007 (Microsoft, Redmond, WA) to generate summary statistics and graphs. We calculated nest success as the percentage of nests classified as "incubating" during the May survey in which at least one eaglet was observed in July. We calculated productivity as the average number of young found in July per nest that was incubating in May. We also calculated the mean number of young found in July per successful nest (i.e., nest with a minimum of one chick present in July). We summarized historic data from 1974-1981, 1983-1988, and 1991-1997 on the location, number, substrate, and productivity of nests located within the Naknek drainage, other drainages within interior KATM, and along the KATM coast. We made rough comparisons between historical and current productivity data using figures and summary statistics. These comparisons must be interpreted with caution as surveys differed in timing, definition of nest status, and study areas (see Discussion for further detail).

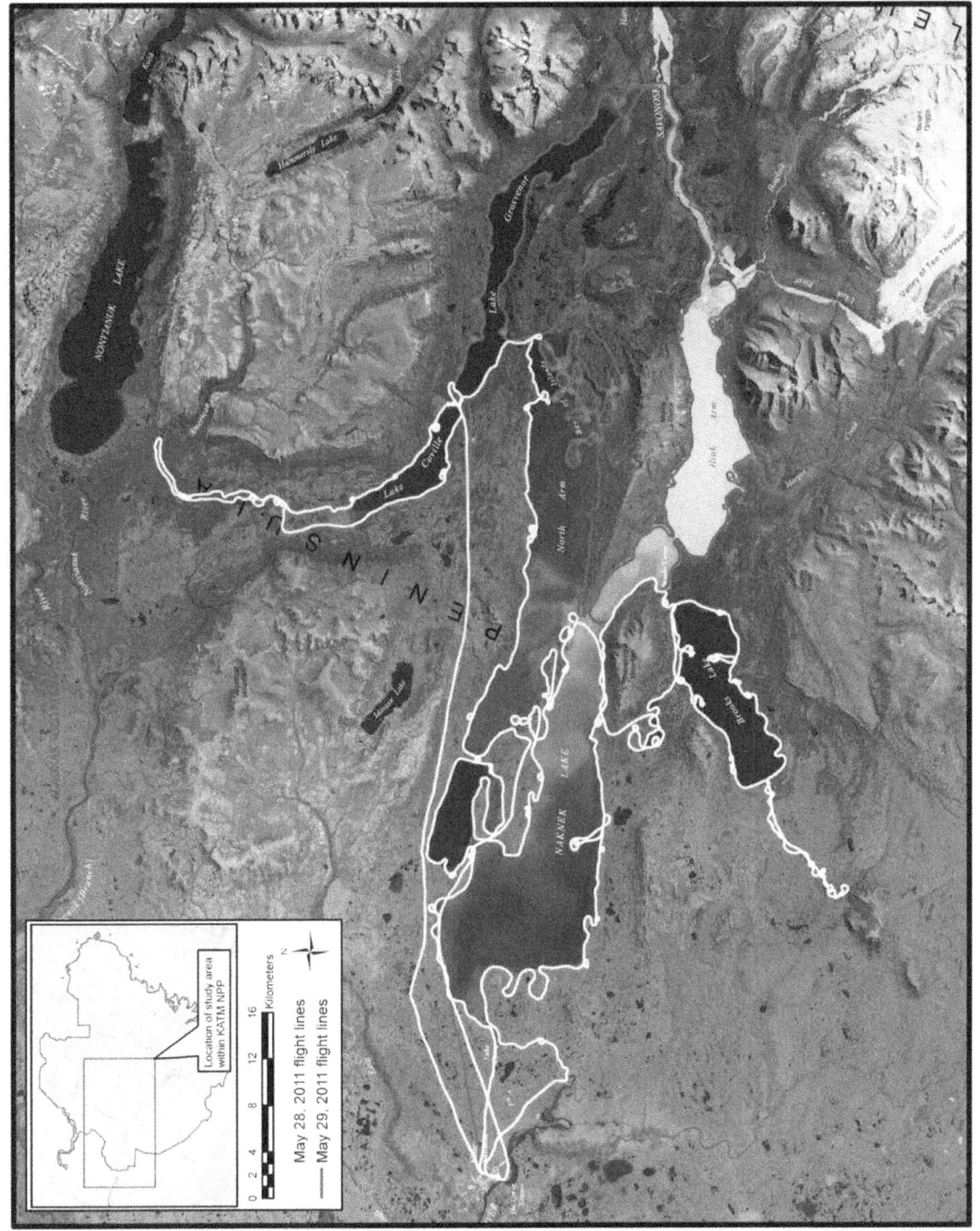

Figure 2. Flight lines from 2011 bald eagle nest occupancy survey of Naknek drainage, KATM.

Table 1. Data collected at each nest detected during aerial surveys for bald eagle nests in the Naknek drainage of KATM during May 28-29, 2011.

Attribute	Codes	Description
Nest ID	NA	A unique number was sequentially assigned to each nest as it was detected. During post-processing nests were given unique ID codes based on the numeric code of the 1:63,360 USGS quadrangle in which they were located.
Observer (front)	0 (not detected), 1 (detected)	Whether or not nest was detected by front-seat observer.
Observer (rear)	0 (not detected), 1 (detected)	Whether or not nest was detected by rear-seat observer.
Number of adults	0, 1, 2, NA	Number of adult eagles seen at or in close vicinity of the nest. Eagles may have been present, but nest classed as "empty" if eagles were not in an incubating posture and eggs/chicks were not present.
Behavior	N (nesting), F (flying), P (perching), NF (nesting and flying), NP (nesting and perching), FP (flying and perching), NA (not applicable)	Behavior of adult eagles observed at/in vicinity of a nest. Two letter codes used when two adult eagles were present.
Nest occupancy	E (empty), I (incubating), NA (not applicable)	Status of detected nest. "Incubating" included nests with an adult eagle present in an incubating posture, eggs present, or chicks present. "Empty" included nests where no adults/eggs/chicks were present, as well as nests where adults were present, but there was no sign that reproduction had occurred.
Nest substrate	S (spruce), C (cottonwood), G (ground), NA (not applicable)	Tree species or substrate where the nest was located. "Ground" included cliffs, hilltops, and any other forms of ground nests.
Tree status	L (live), D (dead), LD (live with large dead branches), NA (not applicable)	Status of tree where nest was located. "NA" if nest was located on the ground.
Tree form	NT (normal complete top), AT (abnormal complete top), BL (broken live top), BD (broken dead top), NA (not applicable)	Further detail on form of tree where nest was located. "NA" if nest was on the ground.

Table 2. Data collected at each nest during aerial survey to determine productivity of bald eagle nests in the Naknek drainage of KATM, July 19, 2011.

Attribute	Codes	Description
Nest productivity status	S (success), F (fail), ND (not determined), NF (not found), NC (not checked)	Status on revisitation of incubating nests found during the initial survey. "Success" included nests with chicks present. "Fail" included empty nests, as well as nests where adults were present without chicks. "Not determined" included nests where foliage, shadows, or other obstructions to visibility prohibited the determination of nest status.
Number of young	0, 1, 2, 3, NA	Number of chicks seen at the nest.
Chick stage	1a (small 1st down), 1b (large 1st down), 2 (2nd down), 3a (early contour), 3b (late contour), 3c (contour with down), 3d (complete contour), ND (not determined), NA.	Stage of chick development based on Carpenter (1990).
Number of adults	0, 1, 2, NA	Number of adult eagles seen at or in close vicinity of the nest.

Results

2011 Survey

We flew an initial survey to determine the location and occupancy of nests within the Naknek drainage on May 28-29, 2011 (Figure 2). Nests with incubating adults present in May were revisited during a follow-up survey on July 19 to determine nesting success and productivity. Total flight time for the initial survey was 8.75 hrs, and 4 hrs for the productivity survey.

During the initial survey we found a total of 58 bald eagle nests; 25 (43%) of which were empty and 33 (57%) with incubating adults present (Figure 3, Appendix A). Of the empty nests, 7 (28%) were located <1 km from a nest with incubating adults. The majority (19) of incubating nests were located on Naknek Lake. Brooks and Coville Lake each had four incubating nests. Two incubating nests were present on Grosvenor Lake, one on American Creek, two on Savonoski/Grosvenor Rivers, and one on Headwaters Creek. Cottonwood (55% of incubating nests) and spruce (45%) were prevalent as nest substrate trees; no ground nests were found in 2011. We attempted to revisit all 33 incubating nests during the productivity survey (Appendix A). We were unable to relocate one nest, and could not determine the productivity status of three additional nests due to foliage and shadows obscuring the nests and limiting visibility. Of the 29 remaining nests, 11 failed (38%) and 18 were successful (62%). There were 0.90 ± 0.15 SE chicks present in July per nest that was classified as incubating in May, and 1.44 ± 0.12 SE chicks per successful nest. Chick development ranged from stage 3a-3c during the productivity survey.

Historical Data

Surveys for eagle nests within the Naknek drainage were conducted periodically between 1974-1997 (Figure 4, Appendix B). Occupancy and productivity surveys were completed in 1975-1979 and 1989-1996; only occupancy surveys were conducted in 1983-1988 and 1997. Number of occupied nests found within the drainage ranged from 5-24 per yr (mean of 13.59 ± 1.30 SE; or 14.67 ± 1.67 SE when data from late June/early July surveys are excluded). Brooks and Naknek Lakes, the largest water bodies within the drainage, traditionally harbored the highest number of occupied nests (Table 3). Cottonwood was the prevalent nest substrate (61.4% of occupied nests ± 3.4 SE), followed by spruce (37.1% ± 3.5 SE; Figure 5). Ground nests were found occasionally (1.5% ± 0.81 SE). Productivity of nests within interior Katmai, including the Naknek drainage, dipped in the mid-1990s, but remained above the level needed to maintain a stable population in all survey years except 1994-1995 (Figures 6-8, Sprunt et al. 1973). Surveys of eagle nesting habitat along the Katmai coast have been conducted less frequently (Figure 9, Appendix B). Production levels along the coast remained above those needed for population stability in three of the four years for which data are available (Figures 10-11).

9

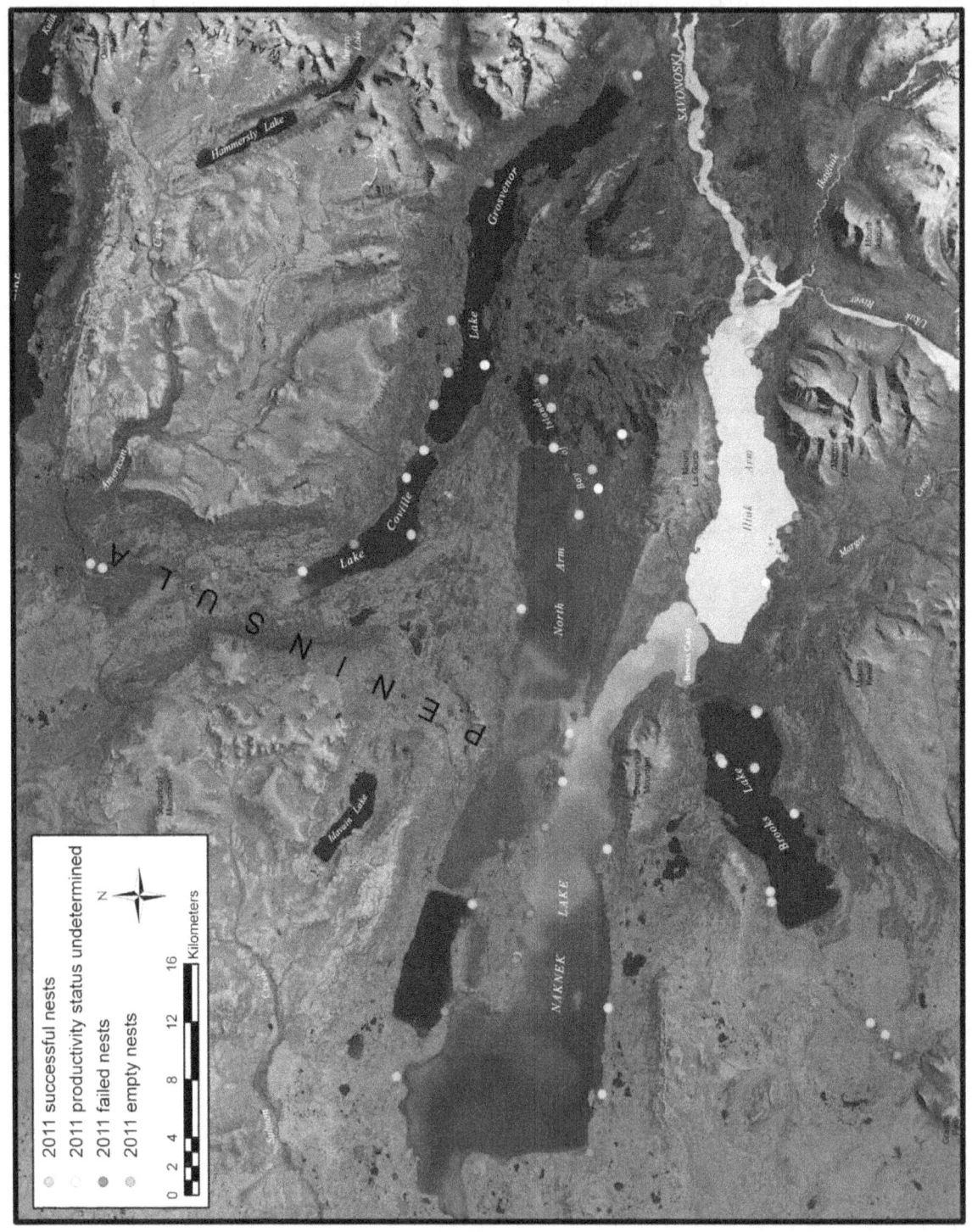

Figure 3. Locations and occupancy/productivity status of bald eagle nests found during surveys of Naknek drainage, KATM in 2011.

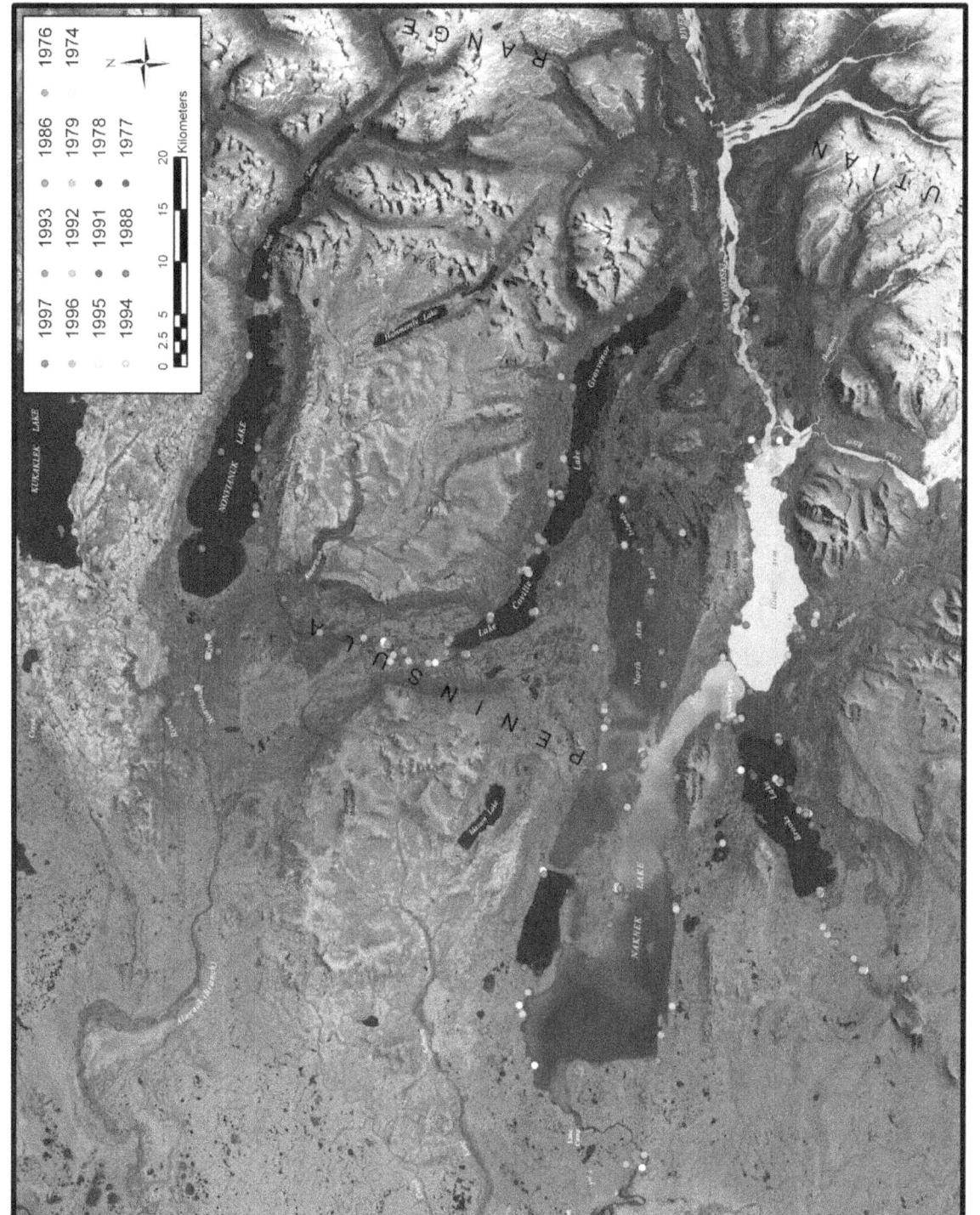

Figure 4. Locations of historically occupied nests found during bald eagle surveys in the interior of KATM.

11

Table 3. Number of occupied nests[1] found during bald eagle nest occupancy surveys[2] on lakes and rivers within the Naknek drainage of KATM during 1975-1981, 1983-1988, 1991-1997, and 2011.

Area	'75	'76	'77	'78	'79	'80	'81	'83	'84	'85	'86	'87	'88	'91	'92	'93	'94	'95	'96	'97	2011[3]
Brooks Lake	0	3	3	4	2	1	3	3	3	1	3	0	3	4	2	1	0	3	1	4	4
Naknek Lake	3	2	6	5	5	2	0	5	1	1	1	4	2[5]	7	8	2	8	5	10	14	19
Coville Lake	0	1	1	1	1	1	0	1	-	4	4	0	-	3	2	3	0	1	1	1	4
Grosvenor Lake	4	4	4	4	4	1	3	1	-	1	0	0	-	0	0	0	1	0	1	1	2
American Creek	1	2	3	3	0	0	1	1	-	0	1	2	2	-	2	2	2	2	3	1	1
Savonoski/ Grosvenor Rvrs	2	5	4	4	3	0	1	2	1	1	3	1	2	1	1	2	1	2	1	3	2
Margot Creek	-	-	-	-	-	-	-	-	-	-	-	-	0	1	-	0	0	1	1	0	0
Headwaters Creek	-	-	-	-	-	-	-	-	-	-	-	-	1	2	3	1	0	2	2	1	1
Total[4]	10	17	21	21	15	5	8	13	-	8	12	7	-	-	15	10	12	16	17	24	32

[1]Historic data from Troyer 1975, Jope 1983-1985, 1987, Dutcher 1986, Squibb 1992, Savage 1993a, 1993b, 1994, 1997.
[2]Occupancy surveys were conducted at varied dates. Comparison of numbers of occupied nests must be made with caution as surveys conducted on later dates may have missed nests that failed early. During 1975-1981, 1993-1997, and 2011, occupancy surveys were conducted between early May and early June. In 1984-1987 and 1991-1992 surveys were conducted in late June or early July. Dates of 1987-1988 surveys are unclear.
[3]2011 data depicts numbers of incubating, as opposed to occupied, nests.
[4]Total does not include nests found in Margot or Headwaters Creeks as these areas were infrequently surveyed.
[5]North arm of Naknek Lake not included in 1988 survey.

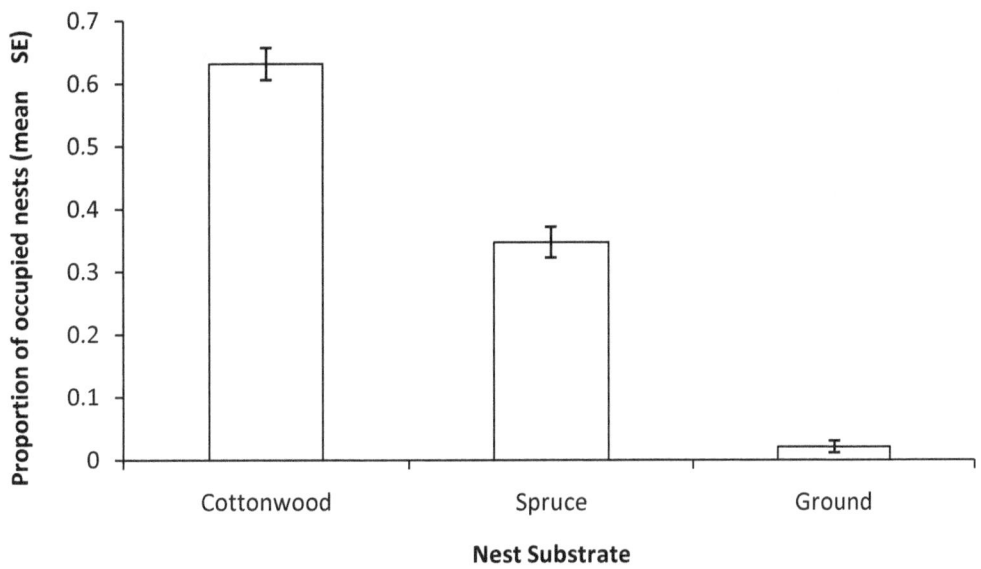

Figure 5. Nest substrate of bald eagle nests in the Naknek drainage area of KATM depicting the proportion ($\bar{x}$ ± SE) of occupied nests of each substrate type detected during occupancy surveys (n=10) conducted during 1974-1979, 1988, and 1991-1997 (data from Troyer 1974-1979, Sowl 1988, and Savage 1993a, b, 1994, 1997).

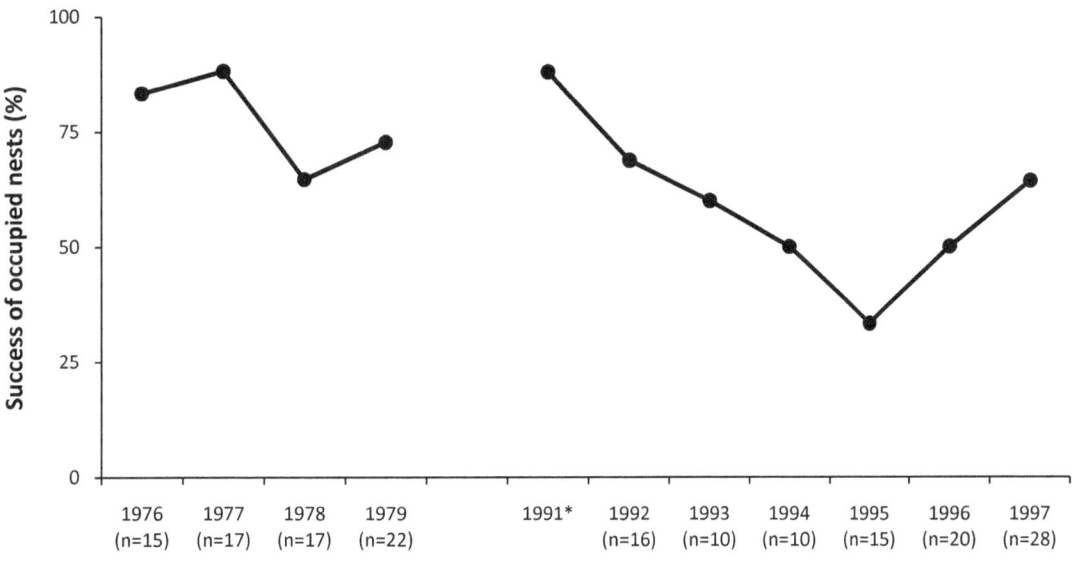

Figure 6. Percent of occupied bald eagle nests successful in interior KATM from 1976-1979 and 1991-1997 (data from Troyer 1976-1979, Squibb 1992, Savage 1993a, b, 1994, 1997). *No information on sample size is available for 1991.

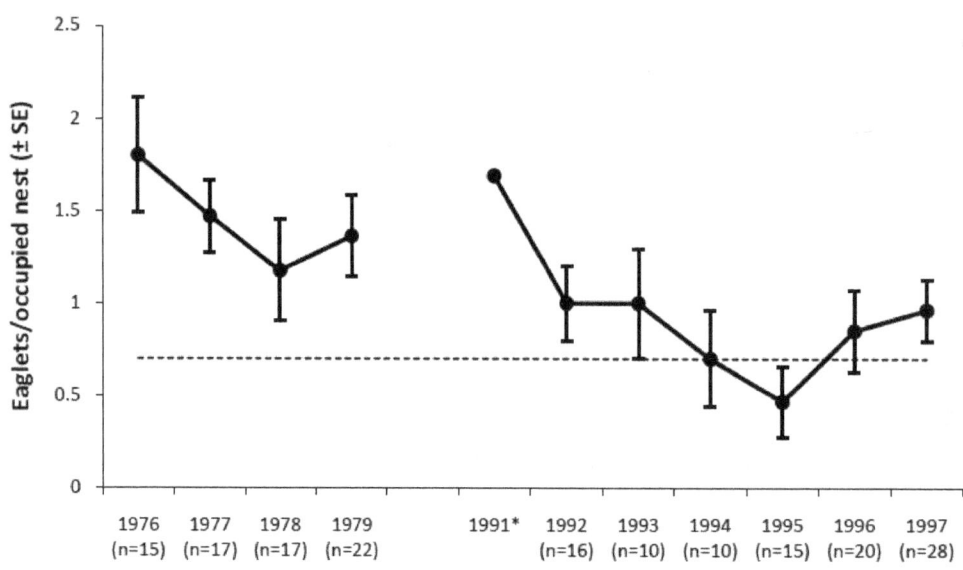

Figure 7. Mean productivity of bald eagle nests in interior KATM from 1976-1979 and 1991-1997 (data from Troyer 1976-1979, Squibb 1992, Savage 1993a, b, 1994, 1997). No information on variation is available for 1991. Dashed line represents minimum needed to maintain a stable population (Sprunt et al. 1973).

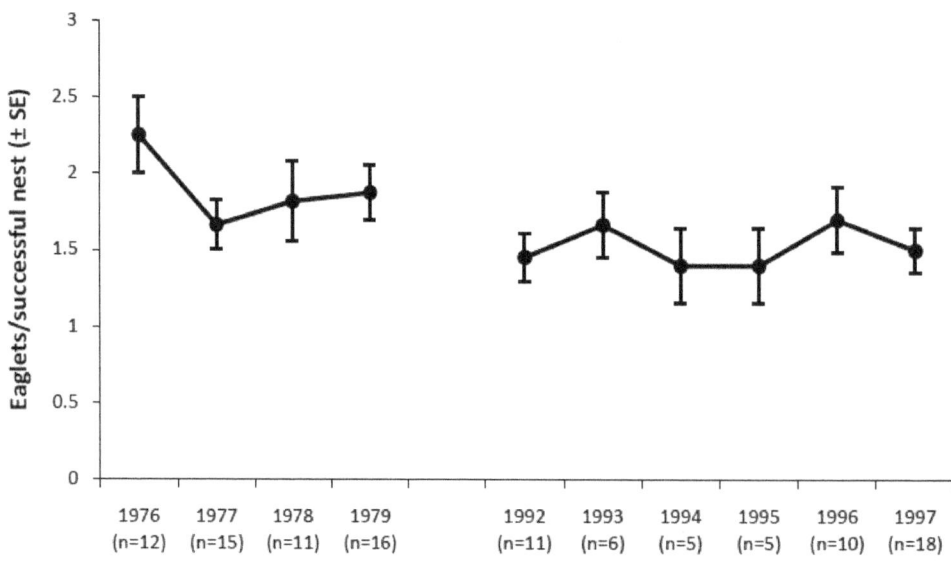

Figure 8. Mean number of eaglets fledged per successful bald eagle nest in interior KATM from 1976-1979 and 1992-1997 (data from Troyer 1976-1979, Savage 1993a, b, 1994, 1997).

Figure 9. Locations of historically occupied nests found during 1974, 1976, 1977, & 1992 bald eagle surveys that included coastal areas of KATM. Locations of a portion of the interior nests found in those survey years are also shown.

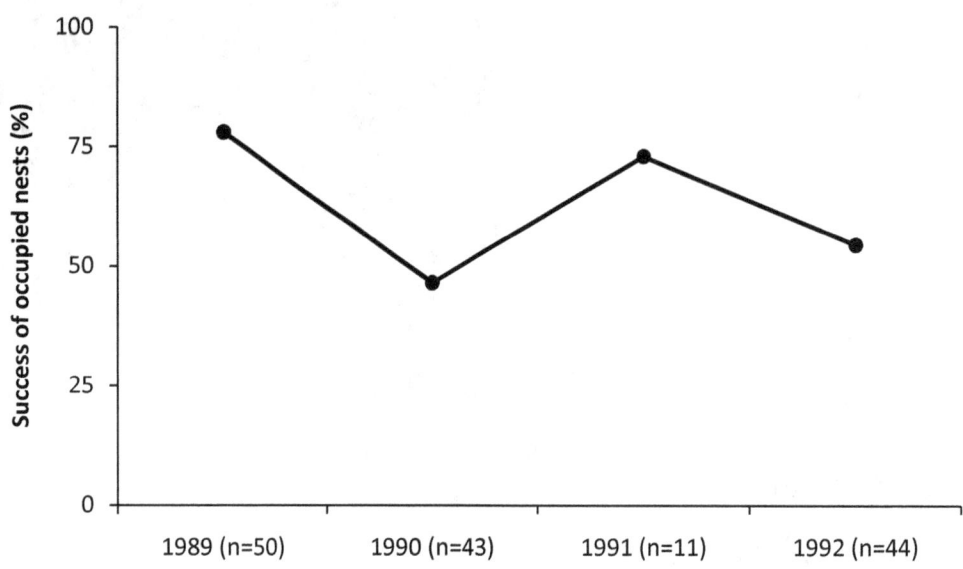

Figure 10. Percent of occupied bald eagle nests successful in coastal KATM from 1989-1992 (data from Yurick 1989, Portner and Schoch 1990, Squibb 1992, Savage 1993a).

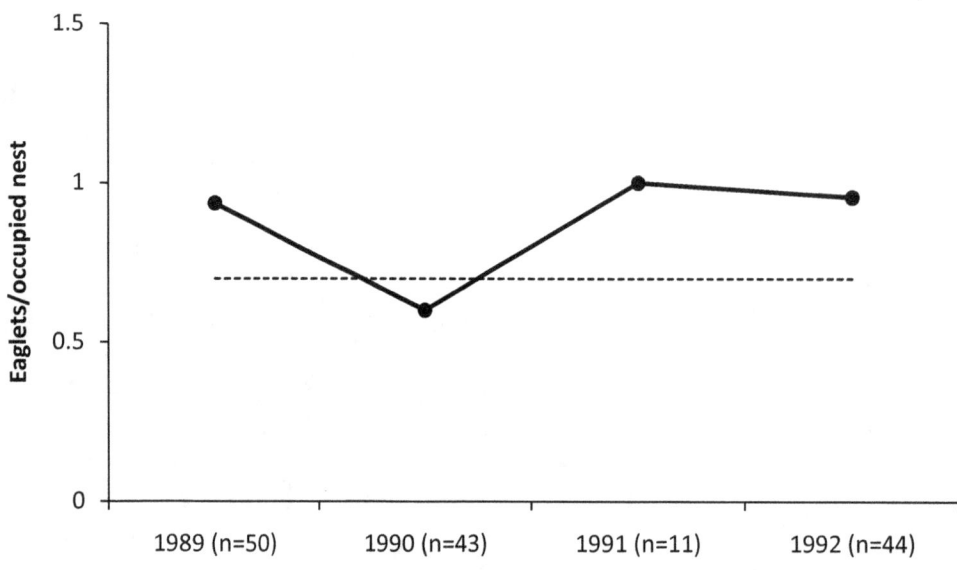

Figure 11. Mean productivity of bald eagle nests in coastal KATM from 1989-1992 (data from Yurick 1989, Portner and Schoch 1990, Squibb 1992, Savage 1993a). No information on variation is available. Dashed line represents minimum needed to maintain a stable population (Sprunt et al. 1973).

Discussion

Results of this study allowed us to meet our primary goals of producing an updated map of incubating and empty bald eagle nests in the Naknek drainage of KATM, as well as comparing current nest occupancy and productivity with past data. This was the first bald eagle nest survey conducted in interior KATM since 1997, and as such was an important initial step for monitoring current and future health of the population. Much work, however, remains to be done to finalize data collection and analysis protocols in order to maximize the usefulness of survey data for biologists and managers at KATM, and to contribute to regional and national monitoring objectives.

The updated map (Figure 3) of bald eagle nests contains 33 incubating nests; the highest number recorded to date for the Naknek drainage. This is the minimum number of incubating nests located in the area. The double-observer sampling method we used will allow us to produce a sightability adjusted estimate of the total number of nests in the area once data analysis protocols are finalized (Thompson et al. 2009, Thompson and Phillips 2011). As in the past, predominant substrates of nests located in 2011 were cottonwood and spruce. Of the 58 nests found in 2011, at least 22 were in the immediate proximity of historic nest sites. Due to imprecision in the mapping of historic locations, we cannot determine whether or not these are exactly the same nest sites that have been used year after year. Nesting success in 2011 was indicative of a stable bald eagle population in the Naknek drainage. This parallels the status of eagle populations along the Alaska Peninsula coast (Savage and Hodges 2000, 2006). Percent nest success, mean number of chicks per incubating nest, and mean number of chicks per successful nest in 2011 fell within the range of productivity rates observed in the past.

Comparisons between 2011 productivity data and data collected from 1974-1997 should be made with caution, however, due to differences in survey timing and definitions of nest status. Our 2011 occupancy survey was conducted in late May, and the majority of past occupancy surveys (1976-1979, 1983-1993) were conducted in late May to late June (Troyer 1976-1979, Jope 1983-1985, 1987, Dutcher 1986, Sowl 1988, Yurick 1989, Portner and Schoch 1990, Squibb 1992, Savage 1993a). While productivity statistics calculated from these data are roughly comparable between years, surveys at these dates may have missed early nest failures resulting in an upward bias in productivity estimates (Postupalsky 1974, Fraser et al. 1983, Bowman et al. 1992). Occupancy surveys were conducted in the first and second weeks of May in 1994-1996, and comparatively lower productivity values may be due to differences in survey timing (Savage 1997). Because of the later occupancy surveys in 1976-1979, 1983-1993, and 2011, productivity values from these years are also inflated estimates when compared to commonly cited metrics in the literature. Sprunt et al. (1973) suggest that nest success greater than 50% and over 0.7 chicks per occupied nest are values indicative of a stable bald eagle population. These metrics were calculated from occupancy surveys conducted near mean egg-laying dates (Sprunt et al. 1973). Comparisons between KATM productivity values and Sprunt et al.'s (1973) metrics suggest the eagle population in KATM has largely been stable or healthy in the past (see Figures 7 & 11). This is likely the case; however, we need to keep in mind the caveat that our productivity measures are skewed high. To facilitate accurate productivity calculations, we suggest that future monitoring efforts follow the recommendation of USFWS Alaska Peninsula/Becharof NWR (2001) to conduct occupancy surveys during the first week of May. This is approximately one week after the mean estimated egg laying date in KATM (Savage 1993b), and corresponds to guidelines for conducting occupancy surveys after at least 90% of clutches have been laid, but before the first broods hatch or a significant number of nest failures occur (Fraser et al. 1983, Bowman 1992, Bowman et al. 1992). This timing would also ensure good nest visibility prior to cottonwood leaf out.

Terminology used to evaluate bald eagle reproductive success is often confusing and different interpretations of data may result (Postupalsky 1974, Bernatowicz et al. 1991). Historical surveys in KATM followed the USFWS nest classification system based on Postupalsky (1974). This system used the categories of empty, occupied, and active to define nest occupancy. Any nest with fresh nesting material or two adults actively defending at or near the nest was considered "occupied" (Savage 1993a, b, 1994, 1997). "Active" was a more restrictive category including only those nests where eggs, chicks, or an adult in an incubating posture were observed. A nest considered "active" in the past surveys is comparable to our "incubating" classification in the 2011 survey. Productivity metrics (percent success, young per incubating nest) calculated in 2011 are skewed higher than past productivity measures because they are calculated using the more restrictive "incubating" classification. On the other hand, measures of the number of young per successful nest are directly comparable between years.

There are both advantages and disadvantages to our current nest occupancy classification scheme. Any inferences made from our work only apply to those nests with eggs or incubating adults detected during the May survey. We chose not to calculate productivity for all "occupied" nests because of several problems inherent in determining nest occupancy. When the presence of two adults at/near a nest is used as the occupancy metric, the issue of incomplete detectability of individuals arises (Bill Thompson, personal communication). This is especially problematic due to the short duration spent at each nest during aerial surveys; a second adult could easily be away from the nest or be present, but not seen (Fraser et al. 1983, Kozie 1993). Proximity distance is another concern when classifying a nest as "occupied" as it is difficult to define the distance from a nest at which point adult eagles are or are not considered to be occupying the nest. By focusing on incubating nests, we avoid the detectability issues mentioned above. A downside of our approach is that many raptor biologists consider the most meaningful measures of reproductive success to be based on occupied nests (Sprunt et al. 1973, Postupalsky 1974, Stalmaster 1987, Bernatowicz et al. 1991). Under a variety of conditions, individual territorial pairs of eagles may refrain from breeding in a given year and we are not able to monitor this type of nest failure using the more restrictive "incubating" classification. In the future, we recommend using the "incubating" definition for modeling trends in nest success in KATM while simultaneously continuing to collect data that fit the broader "occupied" definition. This would require little modification to current data collection methodology and would allow us to maintain a metric that is comparable to past records.

Other major considerations going forward include the study area and scale of future monitoring efforts. Bald eagle nesting habitat is generally defined as sturdy structured trees within one mile of rivers >330 ft wide, water bodies >35 acres, and all coastal areas with suitable nesting structures nearby (USFWS 2009); however, bald eagles in Alaska may also make use of smaller drainages and water bodies (Susan Savage, personal communication). In addition to the Naknek drainage, favorable nesting habitat in KATM is found along the shorelines of Nonvianuk and Kukaklek Lakes and on the coast (Troyer 1975, Sowl 1988, Yurick 1989). Nest occupancy surveys of Nonvianuk Lake were conducted in 1974-1976, 1978-1979, 1983, 1985-1988 (Troyer

1974-1976, 1978-1979, Jope 1983-1985, 1987, Dutcher 1986, Sowl 1988); Kukaklek Lake was surveyed in 1987 (Jope 1987); and, various portions of coastline were studied in 1974-1977, 1989-1990, and 1992 (Troyer 1974-1977, Yurick 1989, Portner and Schoch 1990, Squibb 1992, Savage 1993a). The coast may be particularly important to bald eagles in KATM with roughly 2/3 of the population inhabiting coastal areas in some years (Yurick 1989). ALAG and ANIA, park units administered jointly with KATM, also contain bald eagle nesting habitat. ALAG was surveyed in conjunction with KATM in 1975, 1987, and 1988 (Troyer 1975, Jope 1987, Sowl 1988). Raptor surveys from boat and aircraft have been completed infrequently in coastal ANIA (Starr and Starr 1988, Payer 1989, Dewhurst 1991). Ongoing bald eagle population count and nest occupancy surveys conducted by USFWS at 5-yr intervals also cover a portion of coastal ANIA (Savage and Hodges 2000, 2006). Results of these efforts suggest ANIA offers favorable nesting habitat on cliffs and seastacks (Starr and Starr 1988, Payer 1989).

We recommend expanding future monitoring efforts to include at least portions of coastal KATM, Nonvianuk and Kukaklek Lakes, and ALAG. Initiation of eagle monitoring in ANIA should also be considered. Coast and interior areas of KATM should be treated separately for nest estimation as bald eagle distribution and nest density can vary greatly depending on habitat and other environmental features (USFWS 2009). Bald eagle studies in LACL have documented that year to year variation in nest productivity is not necessarily comparable between coastal and interior areas (Mangipane 2009, Witter and Mangipane 2011). One option at KATM would be to implement a random sampling scheme similar to that used in KEFJ (Thompson and Phillips 2011). An initial survey of all habitat area, following the methods we used to survey the Naknek drainage, would need to be completed for all areas of interest within KATM. Thereafter, randomly selected segments of coast and shoreline could be surveyed on an annual or semi-annual basis; nest occupancy and productivity within these segments could be used to extrapolate parkwide trends. This would yield a more representative sample of eagle habitat throughout the park and provide a broader metric than a nest census conducted in only one area. Another possibility would be to collaborate with USFWS Migratory Birds which currently conducts nest occupancy surveys every 5 yrs in three plots along coastal KATM and two plots in ANIA (Savage and Hodges 2000, 2006). Feasibility of expanded survey efforts needs to be considered with regard to funding, staff, aircraft availability and fuel supply for sampling more remote areas, and safety.

Bald eagles have been selected as a vital sign for long-term monitoring of ecosystem health within SWAN parks, including ALAG, ANIA, KATM, KEFJ, and LACL (Bennett et al. 2006). Data collection methodology is not consistent between the three parks (KATM, KEFJ, and LACL) that have current bald eagle monitoring programs. We based our selection of nest attribute data on KEFJ protocol, but used an ArcPad application similar to that used in LACL. Attribute data collected, however, are very similar between KEFJ and LACL, and can easily be standardized with only minor modifications. KEFJ used an ArcPad application in the past, but found problems with computer speed. We did not experience such problems, but used a simplified application compared to the KEFJ version. Discussion is ongoing over the development of an ArcPad or similar ArcMobile application that could be used in all SWAN units, facilitating data/database management, analysis, and comparison between parks. Simplicity, speed, and ease of use are critical for an application used in the challenging data collection environment of aerial surveys. Users at KATM, KEFJ, and LACL are collaborating to determine key features of a computerized data collection application, and we anticipate implementation of this method in 2012 nest surveys.

Data collection went smoothly during both the occupancy and productivity surveys. We found that programming latitude/longitude of nests to be revisited into the pilot's GPS for the productivity survey facilitated rapid relocation of most nests, as well as efficient transit between nests. Modifications to consider for future survey efforts include increasing the amount of time spent per nest or using two observers during the occupancy survey. We only used one observer with the pilot acting as the second observer, and chose not to photograph nests as we wanted to complete the occupancy survey expeditiously in a limited window of aircraft availability and good weather. However, a photographic record of both empty and occupied nests would be a useful aid for nest relocation in future years. Also, we found it difficult to determine chick stage in some instances during the productivity survey and our classifications should be considered as rough estimates of development. Spending additional time circling each nest or using image-stabilizing binoculars would likely improve the accuracy of developmental classification.

A protocol for analysis of bald eagle nesting data at SWAN parks is currently in the development and testing stage (Thompson et al. 2009, Thompson and Phillips 2011). Efforts to date have centered on a dual-frame approach with double-observer sampling similar to that recommended by the USFWS (2009) for post-delisting monitoring of bald eagles in the lower 48 states. The dual-frame method uses a sample from a list of known nests (i.e., list frame) in combination with additional sampling for new nests in randomly selected segments of eagle habitat (i.e., area frame) to estimate the total number of incubating nests in an area of interest (Haines and Pollock 1998, USFWS 2009, Thompson and Phillips 2011). This method has been shown to detect a larger number of nests with greater precision than monitoring list or area frames on their own (USFWS 2009). The double-observer component allows for estimation of the total number of nests in an area by calculating detection probabilities for each observer to account for nests missed during the survey (Thompson 2004, USFWS 2009). Total number of incubating or occupied nests can be used as an index of bald eagle abundance (USFWS 2009).

Criticisms of dual-frame sampling have been voiced, including concern that it may not be able to detect population changes at desired levels if the list frame decays due to nest turnover or population growth (Watts and Duerr 2010). With this in mind, Thompson and Phillips (2011) suggested the possibility of an alternative approach where the survey is treated as a random sample of segments containing known nests with detection probabilities of 1 and unknown/newly detected nests with detection probabilities <1. Sauer et al. (2011), however, provided a strong argument for dual-frame sampling and addressed concerns over list decay. In balance, the dual-frame method appears effective and logistically feasible. As this design is being used for nationwide monitoring in the lower 48 (USFWS 2009), the benefits of adopting a comparable method in KATM and the other SWAN parks should be considered when weighing values of alternative approaches. Finalizing data analysis protocols will be beneficial in optimizing the allocation of resources to eagle nest surveys. Annual surveys may be necessary in initial years of protocol implementation; however, once several years of data are available, simulations can be used to determine the sampling interval and size of survey area necessary to detect changes in eagle nest occupancy and productivity (Thompson and Phillips 2011).

As keystone predators of waterbirds and fish, bald eagles play a critical role in both freshwater and marine ecosystems. Availability of prey during egg laying and incubation is particularly important (Gende and Wilson 1997, Gende et al. 1997, Elliot et al. 1998, Anthony 2001). Historically, bald eagle nests have been found at the mouths of salmon (*Oncorhynchus* spp.) spawning streams within KATM (Troyer 1974). Population numbers and escapement of salmon, as well as other anadromous fish, may be linked to bald eagle breeding success (Troyer 1975, Anthony 2001). Salmon, however, are not present in interior KATM ecosystems until mid-summer and may be more important to nestling success of interior eagle populations than to nest initiation. Further study into critical food resources during early nesting of eagles in the Naknek drainage is warranted. Weather conditions (Gende et al. 1997) and competition with non-breeding eagles (Hansen 1987) are other natural factors affecting productivity. Potential human-related factors affecting bald eagle breeding success include pollution/contaminants, habitat modification, and increased visitation/disturbance near nesting areas (Yurick 1989, Wiemeyer et al. 1993, Anthony et al. 1994, Gende et al. 1997). Indications are that the eagle population in the Naknek drainage is healthy. Efforts should be put forth to understand factors affecting annual variation in the productivity of this stable population, so we will be better placed to understand causes if productivity declines in the future. Changes in bald eagle nest occupancy and productivity trends over time may indicate that attention needs to be paid to broader natural or human-caused changes occurring within KATM ecosystems.

Literature Cited

Anthony, R.G., R.W. Frenzel, F.B. Isaacs, and M.G. Garrett. 1994. Probable causes of nesting failures in Oregon's Bald Eagle population. Wildlife Society Bulletin 22:576-582.

Anthony, R.G. 2001. Low productivity of bald eagles on Prince of Wales Island, southeast Alaska. The Journal of Raptor Research 35: 1-8.

Armstrong, R.H. 2008. The importance of fish to Bald Eagles in Southeast Alaska: A review. In: Wright, B. A. and P. F. Schempf, eds. Bald Eagles in Alaska. Bald Eagle Research Institute, University of Alaska Southeast, Juneau, Alaska.

Bennett, A. J., W. L. Thompson, and D. C. Mortenson. 2006. Vital signs monitoring plan, Southwest Alaska Network. National Park Service, Anchorage, Alaska. Available from (http://science.nature.nps.gov/im/units/swan/index.cfm?theme=reports_pub). Accessed 3 June 2011.

Bernatowicz, J., T.D. Bowman, and P.F. Schempf. 1991. Bald eagle productivity in southcentral Alaska, 1989 and 1990. USFWS Unpublished Draft Report, Cordova, Alaska.

Bowman, T.D. 1992. Guidelines for conducting bald eagle reproductive surveys in coastal Alaska. USFWS Unpublished Report, Cordova, Alaska.

Bowman, T.D., J.A. Bernatowicz, T.V. Schumacher, and P.F. Schempf. 1992. Bald eagle nesting chronology in Prince William Sound, Alaska, and timing of reproductive surveys. USFWS Unpublished Draft Report, Cordova, Alaska.

Carpenter, G.P. 1990. An illustrated guide for identifying developmental stages of bald eagle nestlings in the field. San Francisco Zoological Society, San Francisco, CA.

Dewhurst, D. 1991. History and status of bald eagle population and productivity studies on the Alaska Peninsula, Alaska. U.S. Fish and Wildlife Service Report, King Salmon, Alaska.

Dutcher, K. 1986. Nesting bald eagle survey Katmai National Park and Preserve – 1986. National Park Service Unpublished Report, King Salmon, Alaska.

Elliot, J.E., I.E. Moul, and K.M. Cheng. 1998. Variable reproductive success of bald eagles on the British Columbia coast. Journal of Wildlife Management 62: 518-529.

Fraser, J.D., L.D. Frenzel, J.E. Mathisen, F. Martin, and M.E. Shough. 1983. Scheduling bald eagle reproductive surveys. Wildlife Society Bulletin 11: 13-16.

Gende, S.M., and M.F. Willson. 1997. Supplemental feeding experiments of nesting bald eagles in southeastern Alaska. Journal of Field Ornithology 68: 590-601.

Gende, S.M., M.F. Wilson, and M. Jacobsen. 1997. Reproductive success of bald eagles (*Haliaeetus leucocephalus*) and its association with habitat or landscape features and weather in southeast Alaska. Canadian Journal of Zoology 75: 1595-1604.

Haines, D.E., and K.H. Pollock. 1998. Estimating the number of active and successful bald eagle nests: an application of the dual frame method. Environmental and Ecological Statistics 5: 245-256.

Hansen, A.J. 1987. Regulation of bald eagle reproductive rates in Southeast Alaska. Ecology 68: 1387-1392.

Hodges, J.I., J.G. King, and F.C. Robard. 1979. Resurvey of Bald Eagle breeding population in southeast Alaska. Journal of Wildlife Management 43: 219-221.

Jope, K.L. 1983. Nesting bald eagle survey Katmai National Park and Preserve – 1983. National Park Service, Natural Resources Survey and Inventory Report AR 83/01, King Salmon, Alaska.

Jope, K.L. 1984. Nesting bald eagle survey Katmai National Park and Preserve – 1984. National Park Service Unpublished Report, King Salmon, Alaska.

Jope, K.L. 1985. Nesting bald eagle survey Katmai National Park and Preserve – 1985. National Park Service Unpublished Report, King Salmon, Alaska.

Jope, K.L. 1987. Nesting bald eagle survey Katmai National Park and Preserve – 1987. National Park Service Unpublished Report, King Salmon, Alaska.

[KATM] Katmai National Park and Preserve. 2009. Katmai National Park and Preserve foundation statement. National Park Service, Anchorage, Alaska.

Kozie, K. 1993, Bald eagle inventory and monitoring plan Wrangell-St. Elias National Park. National Park Service Unpublished Report, Cordova, Alaska.

Kozlowski, J. 2007. Water Resources Information and Issues Overview Report, Katmai National Park and Preserve, Alagnak Wild River. Natural Resource Technical Report NPS/NRPC/WRD/NRTR—2007/057. National Park Service, Fort Collins, Colorado.

Lindsay, C. 2010. Climate monitoring in the Southwest Alaska Network: Annual report for the 2009 hydrologic year. Natural Resource Technical Report NPS/SWAN/NRTR—2010/340. National Park Service, Fort Collins, Colorado.

Mangipane, B.M. 2009. Raptor Populations Inventory – Bald Eagles 2009. National Park Service Unpublished Progress Report, Port Alsworth, AK.

Nichols, J. D., J. E. Hines, J. R. Sauer, F. W. Fallon, J. E. Fallon, and P. J. Heglund. 2000. A double-observer approach for estimating detection probability and abundance from point counts. Auk 117:393-408.

Payer, D.C. 1989. 1989 biological resources survey and oil spill impact assessment: Aniakchak National Preserve. National Park Service Report, King Salmon, Alaska.

Portner, M., and C. Schoch. 1990. Bald eagle nest survey 1990 – Katmai coast. National Park Service Unpublished Report, King Salmon, Alaska.

Postupalsky, S. 1974. Raptor reproductive success: some problems with methods, criteria, and terminology. In: F.N. Hammerstrom, Jr., B.E. Harrel, and R.R. Olendorff, eds. Management of raptors. Raptor Research Foundation, Vermillion, S.D.

Sauer, J.R., M.C. Otto, W.L. Kendall, and G.S. Zimmerman. 2011. Monitoring bald eagles using lists of nests: response to Watts and Duerr. Journal of Wildlife Management 75: 509-512.

Savage, S. 1993a. Bald eagle nesting and productivity, Katmai National Park, 1993. National Park Service Unpublished Report, King Salmon, Alaska.

Savage, S. 1993b. Bald eagle nesting and productivity, Katmai National Park, 1992. National Park Service Unpublished Report, King Salmon, Alaska.

Savage, S. 1994. Bald eagle nesting and productivity, Katmai National Park, 1994. National Park Service Unpublished Report, King Salmon, Alaska.

Savage, S. 1997. Bald eagle nesting and productivity, Katmai National Park, 1995-1997. National Park Service Unpublished Draft Report, King Salmon, Alaska.

Savage, S., and J. Hodges. 2000. Bald eagle survey of the Pacific coast of the Alaska Peninsula, Alaska, spring 2000. U.S. Fish and Wildlife Service, King Salmon, Alaska.

Savage, S., and J. Hodges. 2006. Bald eagle survey of the Pacific coast of the Alaska Peninsula, Alaska, spring 2005. U.S. Fish and Wildlife Service, King Salmon, Alaska.

Sowl, K. 1988. Bald eagle survey – 1988. National Park Service Unpublished Report, King Salmon, Alaska.

Sprunt, A., W.B. Robertson, Jr., S. Postupalsky, R.J. Hensel, C.E. Knoder, and F.J. Ligas. 1973. Comparative productivity of six Bald Eagle populations. Trans. N. Am. Wildl. Nat. Res. Conf. 38:96-106.

Squibb, R. 1992. Bald eagle nesting and productivity, Katmai National Park, 1991. National Park Service Unpublished Report, King Salmon, Alaska.

Stalmaster, M.V. 1987. The bald eagle. Universe Books, New York, NY.

Starr, F., and P. Starr. 1988. 1988 coastal raptor survey Aniakchak National Monument and Preserve. National Park Service Unpublished Report, King Salmon, Alaska.

Swenson, J.E., K.L. Alt, and R.L. Eng. 1986. Ecology of bald eagles in the Greater Yellowstone ecosystem. Wildlife Monographs 85: 3-46.

Thompson, W.L. 2004. Sampling Rare or Elusive Species. Island Press., Washington, DC.

Thompson, W. L., S. Hall, and C. R. Lindsay. 2009. Evaluation of a survey method for estimating and monitoring the number of active bald eagle nests in Kenai Fjords National Park. Natural Resource Technical Report NPS/SWAN/NRTR—2009/271. National Park Service, Fort Collins, Colorado.

Thompson, W. L., and L. M. Phillips. 2011. Evaluation of a dual-frame design to estimate occupancy and productivity of bald eagle nests in Kenai Fjords National Park. Natural Resource Technical Report NPS/SWAN/NRTR—2011/413. National Park Service, Fort Collins, Colorado.

Troyer, W. 1974. Distribution and density of bald eagle nests Katmai area, Alaska. National Park Service, Alaska Region, Natural Resources Survey and Inventory Report AR 74/02.

Troyer, W. 1975. Distribution and density of bald eagle nests Katmai - 1975. National Park Service, Alaska Region, Natural Resources Survey and Inventory Report AR 75/04.

Troyer, W. 1976. Nesting and productivity of bald eagles Katmai - 1976. National Park Service, Alaska Region, Natural Resources Survey and Inventory Report AR 76/03.

Troyer, W. 1977. Nesting and productivity of bald eagles Katmai - 1977. National Park Service, Alaska Region, Natural Resources Survey and Inventory Report AR 77/01.

Troyer, W. 1978. Nesting and productivity of bald eagles Katmai - 1978. National Park Service, Alaska Region, Natural Resources Survey and Inventory Report AR 78/01.

Troyer, W. 1979. Nesting and productivity of bald eagles Katmai - 1979. National Park Service, Alaska Region, Natural Resources Survey and Inventory Report AR 79/01.

USFWS. 2009. Post-delisting Monitoring Plan for the Bald Eagle (*Haliaeetus leucocephalus*) in the Contiguous 48 States. U.S. Fish and Wildlife Service, Divisions of Endangered Species and Migratory Birds and State Programs, Midwest Regional Office, Twin Cities, Minnesota.

USFWS Alaska Peninsula/Becharof NWR. 2001. Draft Wildlife Inventory Plan: Alaska Peninsula/Becharof National Wildlife Refuge Complex. Unpublished Document, King Salmon, Alaska.

Watts, B.D., and A.E. Duerr. 2010. Nest turnover rates and list-frame decay in bald eagles: implications for the national monitoring plan. Journal of Wildlife Management 75: 940-944.

Wiemeyer, S. N., C. M. Bunck, and C. J. Stafford. 1993. Environmental contaminants in bald eagle eggs 1980-84 and further interpretations of relationships to productivity and shell thickness. Archives of Environmental Contamination and Toxicology 24:213-227.

Witter, L.A., and B.M. Mangipane. 2011. Bald eagle nest survey in Lake Clark National

Park and Preserve, Alaska. Natural Resource Data Series NPS/LACL/NRDS—2011/XXX.
National Park Service, Fort Collins, Colorado.

Yurick, M.M. 1989. 1989 raptor nest inventory and productivity survey Katmai National
Park and Preserve. National Park Service Unpublished Report, King Salmon, Alaska.

Appendix A: Bald eagle nest data from 2011 occupancy & productivity surveys, Naknek drainage, KATM.

Attributes of nests located during the 2011 bald eagle early occupancy survey and status during late productivity survey, Naknek drainage, KATM, Alaska. See Tables 1 & 2 for definitions of codes used to describe nest attributes.

Nest ID	Location	Substrate	Tree Status	Tree Form	Observer (front)	Observer (rear)	# Adults (occup.)	Behavior	Occup.	Product.	# Young	Chick stage	# Adults (product.)
114-45-03	American Crk	C	L	NT	1	1	1	N	I	F	0	NA	0
113-21-01	Brooks Lk	S	L	NT	0	1	1	N	I	S	1	3a	1
114-26-01	Brooks Lk	S	L	NT	0	1	1	N	I	S	1	3a	1
114-36-07	Brooks Lk	S	L	NT	1	1	1	N	I	S	2	3a	2
114-36-10	Brooks Lk	S	L	NT	1	1	2	NP	I	S	1	3a	1
114-34-02	Grosvenor Rvr	C	L	NT	1	1	2	NP	I	S	2	3a	0
113-21-05	Headwaters Crk	C	L	NT	0	1	1	N	I	F	0	NA	0
114-35-02	LK Coville	S	L	NT	1	0	1	N	I	S	1	3a	1
114-35-03	Lk Coville	S	D	NT	1	1	1	N	I	S	1	3a	1
114-45-04	Lk Coville	S	L	NT	1	1	2	NP	I	S	1	ND	1
114-45-05	Lk Coville	S	LD	BD	1	1	1	N	I	F	0	NA	0
114-34-01	Lk Grosvenor	C	L	NT	1	1	2	NP	I	F	0	NA	0
114-35-07	Lk Grosvenor	C	L	NT	1	0	1	N	I	ND	NA	NA	1
113-31-02	Naknek Lk	S	L	NT	1	1	2	NP	I	F	0	NA	0
113-31-04	Naknek Lk	C	L	NT	1	1	1	N	I	F	0	NA	0
113-31-07	Naknek Lk	C	L	NT	1	0	1	N	I	F	0	NA	0
113-31-08	Naknek Lk	C	L	NT	1	1	1	N	I	S	2	3a	1
113-31-09	Naknek Lk	C	L	NT	1	1	1	N	I	S	2	3c	1
113-32-01	Naknek Lk	S	L	NT	0	1	1	N	I	F	0	NA	0
114-25-01	Naknek Lk	C	L	NT	0	1	2	NP	I	F	0	NA	0
114-25-02	Naknek Lk	S	L	NT	1	1	1	N	I	F	0	NA	0
114-35-10	Naknek Lk	C	L	NT	1	1	1	N	I	S	1	3c	1
114-35-12	Naknek Lk	C	L	NT	1	0	1	N	I	NF	NA	NA	NA
114-35-13	Naknek Lk	C	L	NT	1	1	2	NP	I	ND	NA	NA	1
114-35-14	Naknek Lk	C	L	NT	1	1	2	NP	I	S	2	3a	1
114-35-15	Naknek Lk	S	L	NT	1	1	1	N	I	S	1	3c	1
114-35-18	Naknek Lk	S	L	NT	1	1	1	N	I	ND	NA	NA	1

114-36-01	Naknek Lk	S	L	NT	1	1	1	N	I	F	0	NA	0
114-36-02	Naknek Lk	S	D	NT	0	1	1	N	I	S	1	3c	0
114-36-03	Naknek Lk	C	L	NT	1	1	1	N	I	S	2	3a	2
114-36-04	Naknek Lk	C	L	NT	0	1	1	N	I	S	2	3a	1
114-36-11	Naknek Lk	C	L	NT	1	0	1	N	I	S	2	3b	1
114-34-05	Savonoski Rvr	C	L	NT	1	1	2	NP	I	S	1	3b	2
114-45-01	American Crk	C	L	NT	1	0	0	NA	E	NA	NA	NA	NA
114-45-02	American Crk	C	L	NT	1	0	0	NA	E	NA	NA	NA	NA
113-21-02	Brooks Lk	S	L	NT	1	1	0	NA	E	NA	NA	NA	NA
114-36-05	Brooks Lk	S	D	NT	1	0	0	NA	E	NA	NA	NA	NA
114-36-06	Brooks Lk	S	L	NT	0	1	0	NA	E	NA	NA	NA	NA
114-36-08	Brooks Lk	C	L	AT	1	1	0	NA	E	NA	NA	NA	NA
114-36-09	Brooks Lk	S	L	NT	1	1	0	NA	E	NA	NA	NA	NA
113-21-03	Headwaters Crk	S	D	NT	1	0	0	NA	E	NA	NA	NA	NA
113-21-04	Headwaters Crk	C	L	NT	0	1	0	NA	E	NA	NA	NA	NA
114-35-01	Lk Coville	C	L	NT	1	0	0	NA	E	NA	NA	NA	NA
114-35-04	Lk Grosvenor	S	D	NT	1	1	0	P	E	NA	NA	NA	NA
114-35-05	Lk Grosvenor	C	L	NT	1	1	2	NA	E	NA	NA	NA	NA
114-35-06	Lk Grosvenor	C	L	NT	1	0	0	NA	E	NA	NA	NA	NA
113-31-01	Naknek Lk	S	L	NT	0	1	0	NA	E	NA	NA	NA	NA
113-31-03	Naknek Lk	C	L	NT	1	0	0	NA	E	NA	NA	NA	NA
113-31-05	Naknek Lk	C	L	NT	1	0	0	NA	E	NA	NA	NA	NA
113-31-06	Naknek Lk	C	D	NT	1	0	0	NA	E	NA	NA	NA	NA
114-35-08	Naknek Lk	C	L	NT	1	0	0	NA	E	NA	NA	NA	NA
114-35-09	Naknek Lk	S	L	NT	1	1	2	P	E	NA	NA	NA	NA
114-35-11	Naknek Lk	C	L	NT	1	0	0	NA	E	NA	NA	NA	NA
114-35-16	Naknek Lk	C	L	NT	1	0	0	NA	E	NA	NA	NA	NA
114-35-17	Naknek Lk	C	L	NT	1	0	0	NA	E	NA	NA	NA	NA
114-34-03	Savonoski Rvr	S	L	NT	1	0	0	NA	E	NA	NA	NA	NA
114-34-04	Savonoski Rvr	C	L	NT	1	1	0	NA	E	NA	NA	NA	NA
114-34-06	Savonoski Rvr	C	L	NT	1	0	0	NA	E	NA	NA	NA	NA

Appendix B: Available documentation for bald eagle surveys 1974-1997, KATM.

Summary of bald eagle surveys conducted from 1974-1997 in KATM.

Year	Dates	Type	Area	Documentation
1974	May 15 (interior) Jun 1-2 (coast)	occupancy	Naknek Lk drainage Kulik Lk drainage S. shore Nonvianuk Lk coast McNeil Rvr to Cape Aklek	Troyer 1974
1975	May 14, 15, 19, 23 Aug 4-5	occupancy productivity	Douglas & Kamishak drainages American Rvr drainage Alagnak Rvr/Nonvianuk drainage coast Wide Bay to Katmai	Troyer 1975
1976	late May Jul 31, Aug 1	occupancy productivity	Douglas & Kamishak drainages American Rvr drainage Kulik Lk drainage Nonvianuk Lk drainage coast to Cape Aklek	Troyer 1976
1977	late May early Aug	occupancy productivity	Douglas & Kamishak drainages American Rvr drainage coast from Cape Douglas to Puale Bay	Troyer 1977
1978	late May early Aug	occupancy productivity	Douglas & Kamishak drainages American Rvr drainage Kulik Lk drainage Nonvianuk Lk drainage	Troyer 1978
1979	late May late Jul/early Aug	occupancy productivity	Douglas & Kamishak drainages American Rvr drainage Kulik Lk drainage Nonvianuk Lk drainage	Troyer 1979
1983	Jul 2-3	occupancy	Brooks & Naknek Lks Coville & Grosvenor Lks Nonvianuk & Kulik Lks	Jope 1983

Year	Date	Parameter	Location	Reference
1984	Jul 7	occupancy	Brooks & Naknek Lks, Savonoski & Grosvenor Rvrs, American Rvr drainage	Jope 1984
1985	Jul 4-6	occupancy	Brooks & Naknek Lks, Coville & Grosvenor Lks, Nonvianuk & Kulik Lks, Savonoski & Grosvenor Rvrs, American Rvr drainage	Jope 1985
1986	Jun 29, Jul 3-4	occupancy	Brooks & Naknek Lks, Coville & Grosvenor Lks, Nonvianuk & Kulik Lks, Savonoski & Grosvenor Rvrs, American Rvr drainage	Dutcher 1986
1987	Jun 30-Jul 3	occupancy	Brooks & Naknek Lks, Coville & Grosvenor Lks, Nonvianuk & Kulik Lks, Kukaklek Lk, Savonoski & Grosvenor Rvrs, American Rvr drainage, Alagnak & Nonvianuk Rvrs	Jope 1987
1988	May 28-29	occupancy	Brooks & Naknek Lks, Nonvianuk Lk, Headwaters & Margot Crks, Savonoski & Rainbow Rvrs, Alagnak & Nonvianuk Rvrs, American Rvr drainage	Sowl 1988
1989	Jun 11, Aug 13	occupancy, productivity	entire coast	Yurick 1989
1990	May 26-27, Jul 24-25	occupancy, productivity	coast Cape Kubagakli to Kamishak Bay	Portner & Schoch 1990

Year	Dates	Type	Locations	Reference
1991	Jun 12-13, 21 Jul 10	occupancy productivity	Brooks & Naknek Lks Coville & Grosvenor Lks Savonoski Rvr Headwaters Crk Amalik Bay	Squibb 1992
1992	Jun 10, 12, 24-25 (Naknek) May 31, Jun 1 (coast) Jul 24 (Naknek) Jul 20-21 (coast)	occupancy productivity	Brooks & Naknek Lks Coville & Grosvenor Lks Hamersley Lk Savonoski Rvr Headwaters Crk coast Cape Kubagakli to Kamishak Bay	Savage 1993a
1993	May 12, 20 Jul 22	occupancy productivity	Brooks & Naknek Lks Coville & Grosvenor Lks Savonoski & Grosvenor Rvrs Headwaters & Margot Crks American Rvr drainage	Savage 1993b
1994	May 6, 9 Jul 25	occupancy productivity	Brooks & Naknek Lks Coville & Grosvenor Lks Savonoski & Grosvenor Rvrs Headwaters & Margot Crks American Rvr drainage	Savage 1994
1995	May 9, 12 Jul 19	occupancy productivity	Brooks & Naknek Lks Coville & Grosvenor Lks Savonoski & Grosvenor Rvrs Headwaters & Margot Crks American Rvr drainage	Savage 1997
1996	May 6, 10 Jul 22	occupancy productivity	Brooks & Naknek Lks Coville & Grosvenor Lks Savonoski & Grosvenor Rvrs Headwaters & Margot Crks American Rvr drainage	Savage 1997
1997	May 6, 7 Jul 23	occupancy productivity	Brooks & Naknek Lks Coville & Grosvenor Lks	Savage 1997

Savonoski & Grosvenor Rvrs
Headwaters & Margot Crks
American Rvr drainage

www.ingramcontent.com/pod-product-compliance
Lightning Source LLC
Chambersburg PA
CBHW080918290526
45795CB00007BA/2569